LIBRARY
LONGFELLOW ELEMENTARY SCHOOL

JANE LONG
Frontier Woman

by
Ann Fears Crawford
Illustrated by Rosario Baxter
W.S. Benson & Company • Austin, Texas

FIRST EDITION

Text copyright © 1990 by Ann Fears Crawford
Illustrations copyright © 1990 by Rosario Baxter

Published in the United States of America
by W.S. Benson & Co., P.O. Box 1866, Austin, Texas 78767

ALL RIGHTS RESERVED. No part of this book may be reproduced in any form without written permission from the publisher, except for brief passages included in a review appearing in a newspaper or magazine.

ISBN 0-87443-090-9
Library of Congress Cataloging-in-Publication Data
Crawford, Ann Fears.
    Jane Long—Frontier Woman/by Ann Fears Crawford: Illustrated by Rosario Baxter.
    p. 60 cm. 24
    Bibliography: p. 60
    Summary: A biography of Jane Long, "Mother of Texas," her life and adventures in the Republic of Texas.
    ISBN 0-87443-090-9: $12.95
    1. Long, Jane, 1798-1880—Juvenile literature. 2. Women pioneers—Texas—Juvenile literature. 3. Frontier and pioneer life—Texas—Juvenile literature. (l. Long, Jane, 1798-1880. 2. Women pioneers. 3. Frontier and pioneer life).
I. Baxter, Rosario, Ill. II. Title.
F389.L6C73   1990
976.4'04'
(B)   CIP   89-82685
                                                                   AC

for
Mayes Middleton
young Texas historian

DREAMS OF ADVENTURE

Many people came to frontier Texas. Many came looking for land and adventure. Some dreamed of empires in early Texas. Others came to make their fortunes.

Most came to find good land and new homes on the frontier.

Jane Long came to Texas with her husband. Dr. James Long dreamed of an empire in Texas. Jane dreamed of adventure also.

She found a life of adventure in Texas, but she also found many hardships.

Jane's uncle was a brave adventurer. James Wilkinson had been a soldier in the Revolutionary War. Then he met Aaron Burr. The two men planned to take Louisiana away from Spain.

Then Wilkinson became alarmed. He might be called a traitor. He told President Thomas Jefferson of the plot. Burr was captured, but Wilkinson went free.

Still James Wilkinson dreamed of an empire in Mexico.

When Jane's father died, her mother took her to Mississippi. There Jane's uncle told her tales of his bold adventures. He told Jane his dreams. And he treated Jane as his own daughter.

Jane was happy at her uncle's home. She learned to read and write. She also learned to spin and weave.

Jane spent many hours making quilts and dreaming of adventures in faraway lands.

FALLING IN LOVE

When Jane was sixteen, she met her own bold adventurer.

One day she was late to school. But her maid Kian told her to wait. A visitor was coming. Dr. James Long had been called to treat a wounded soldier.

Kian knew that Jane would like the handsome soldier.

The young couple played a game. James bet Jane he would win at backgammon. When James lost, he gave Jane a reward—a beautiful pair of white gloves.

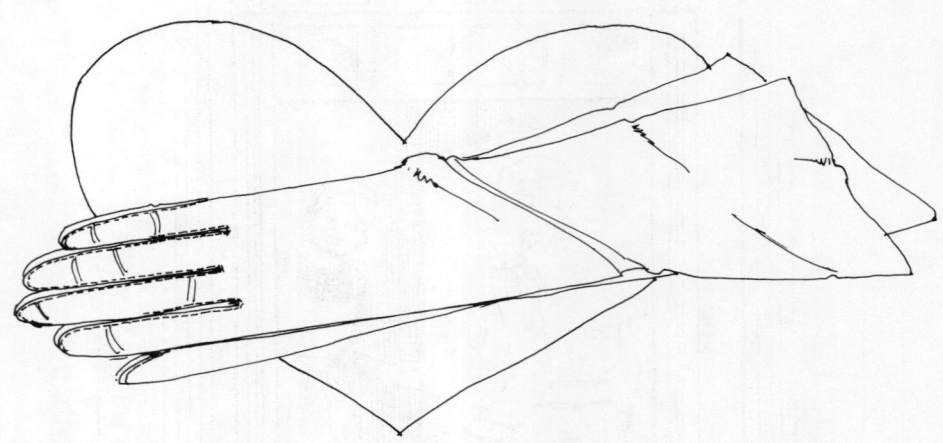

Soon Jane knew she was in love with her handsome soldier. But her uncle refused to let them marry.

Jane pleaded with him. But General Wilkinson did not want his niece to marry a soldier.

He knew how hard a soldier's life was. And he knew how often a soldier's wife would be alone.

James talked to the general. He told him he would leave the army. Still the general would not agree.

Then Jane had an idea. Soon she would be eighteen. She had no father. James was five years older than she was. He could be her guardian.

Then James could grant her the right to be married.

On May 14, 1815 the young couple married, and James left the army. He and Jane moved to Port Gibson where he practiced medicine.

But Jane did not like living in a small town. So James became a planter.

When their first child was born, Jane and James were very happy. They named their daughter Ann Herbert.

But James was not happy as a planter. He tried being a merchant.

Still he longed for a life of adventure.

Texas—Land of Adventure

Across the United States people were talking about the West. Over the Sabine River lay rich land.

Explorers and traders brought back stories of a land of adventure—Texas.

Between Texas and Louisiana lay the Neutral Ground. Spain owned Texas, but no one knew who owned the Neutral Ground.

Here was an empire for the taking thought James Long!

Texas belonged to Spain. But James thought he could take it from the Spaniards. He could claim Texas for his own.

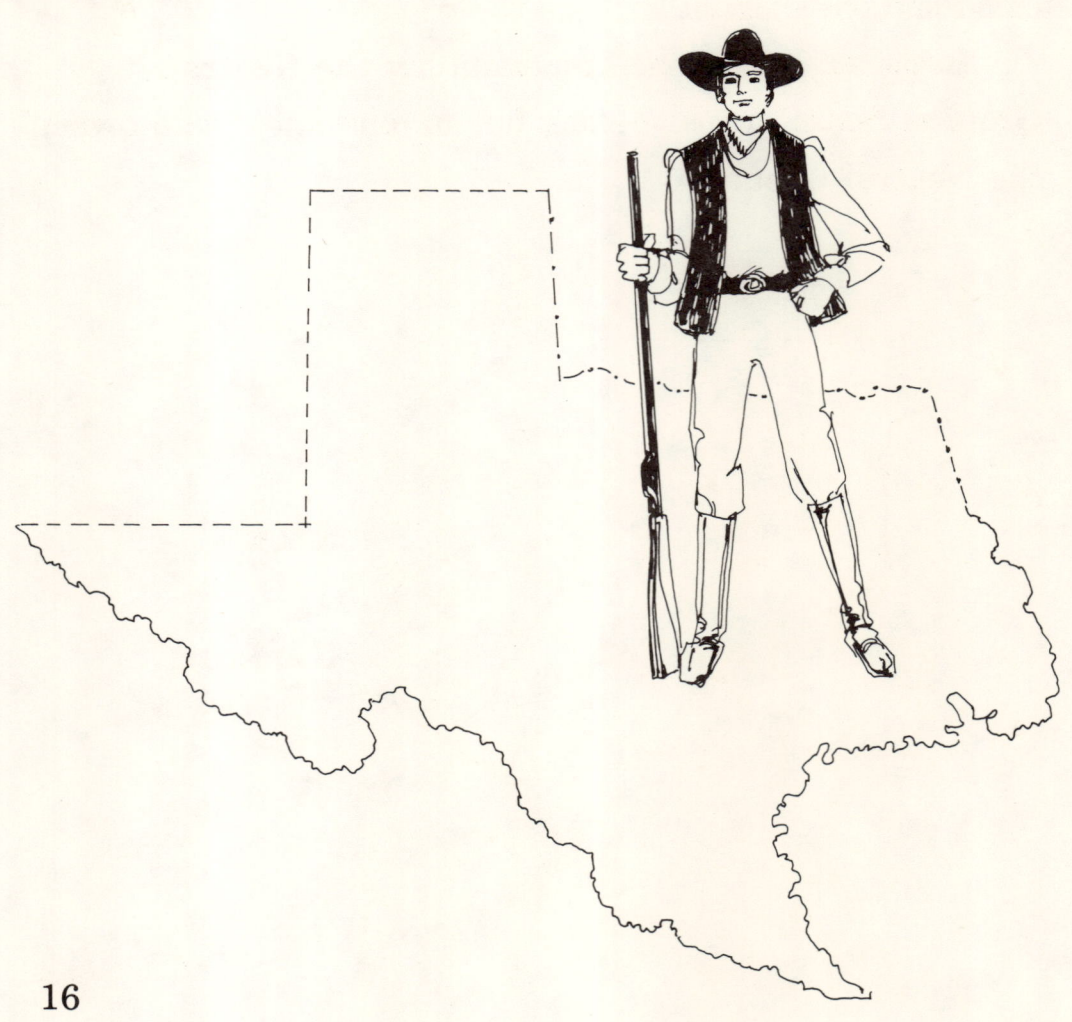

Men listened to James Long. Many thought Texas should be free. Others thought Texas should be part of the United States. Some wanted to march to Texas and take it.

Many people gave money for an army. Men joined. They chose James Long as their leader.

Jane wanted to go with her husband. But James wanted her to wait. She was going to have another child.

Still Jane did her part. She sewed a flag for the army. It was white silk with red stripes. Jane sewed gold fringe on her flag. How proud she was to see her flag flying at the head of James's army.

James promised to fly Jane's flag in Texas. Then he kissed her goodbye. They both knew they would not see one another for a very long time.

Jane had to wait. She was very lonely and missed her husband.

But soon she had a new baby to keep her company. She named their new daughter Rebecca.

Jane wanted to join her James in Texas.

Then she had a letter from her husband. James and his army were in Nacogdoches.

James flew Jane's flag over the Old Stone Fort. James Long had won his empire in Texas.

OFF TO TEXAS!

Soon Jane was packing. She was on her way to join James.

She kissed her new baby and left her with her sister. She knew the journey would be too hard for young Rebecca.

Kian and young Ann went with Jane. Other men and women went also. They traveled day and night. Often their mules stumbled through streams. Their carriage wheels stuck in the mud.

Jane was very happy to reach East Texas. Soon the travelers reached Nacogdoches. Jane saw her flag flying bravely in the breeze.

Then she saw James. He was running to greet her. She raced into his arms. How happy they were—together at last in Texas!

Then Jane had sad news. Her baby Rebecca had died. James tried to comfort his wife. He wanted to stay with her and Ann in East Texas.

But the Spanish army was on the march. Texas belonged to Spain, and the Spanish army was going to keep it. They wanted James Long and his army out of Texas.

James knew he needed help against the Spaniards. He knew who might aid him. The pirate Jean Lafitte roamed Galveston Island. Perhaps he might march with James against the Spaniards.

James took his family to Bolivar Point. It was on Galveston Bay. He hated to leave Jane alone for she was going to have another baby.

James needed money for his army. Once again he kissed Jane goodbye. She and Ann would wait for him at Bolivar Point.

Jane had Kian for company. She also had a little dog they called "Galveston."

The other settlers were afraid. They were afraid of the Indians that roamed nearby. They were also afraid the Spaniards might attack.

The settlers packed their belongings. They were leaving. They begged Jane to come with them.

"No," Jane said. "My husband left me here. I'll wait for him."

A Lonely Christmas

Then winter came. Snow fell. Ice covered the ground. Even Galveston Bay was frozen.

Jane and Kian cut holes in the ice. "Galveston" tagged along with them. The two women caught fish for their supper. They shot birds and gathered oysters.

One day Jane spotted a large fish. If only she could catch it. She dropped her hook into the water. The fish bit.

Then the hook broke. Jane's fish swam away. Jane almost cried. Now they would have no supper.

The fort was not a good shelter in cold weather. The wind blew through the cracks. Snow swirled around the door. Even "Galveston" shivered with cold.

Jane and her family took shelter in a tent. Then Kian fell ill, and Jane had no one to help her.

"Galveston" whined for his dinner. Jane picked up her fishing pole and went out to fish. She caught a big fish for their supper.

When Jane cut the fish open, there was the fish hook she had lost. She had caught her prize fish. Everyone enjoyed a special dinner.

Even though it was cold, Jane was very happy. She lay on her pallet covered with snow. Now she had the nicest Christmas present of all.

She smiled at her new baby girl. Here was a new Texan to please her husband.

Jane named her new baby Mary James. How proud James would be to have his daughter have his name.

Then a cold storm blew in. Food was hard to find. Jane and Ann searched for frozen fish on the beach.

Some they had for their Christmas dinner. The rest they stored in a pickle barrel.

INDIANS!

Soon Kian was well. One day she went to gather oysters. "Galveston" trotted along with her.

Suddenly "Galveston" barked and barked. He began running around in circles.

Kian looked up. She spotted a canoe rounding the bend. Indians were paddling straight for Bolivar Point.

Kian dropped her sack. She screamed, and Jane came running. The two women acted quickly.

Kian sprang for the cannon. Jane took off her red flannel petticoat. She ran it up the flagpole.

The women fired the cannon. Cannonballs hurled out over Galveston Bay.

Suddenly the canoe stopped. The Indians thought soldiers were at the fort. Slowly the canoe turned around. Danger was over!

Still Jane and Kian were on guard. They were afraid the Indians would return.

Every day Jane fired the cannon. She hoped the cannon's boom would keep the Indians away.

Kian wore a soldier's uniform when she gathered oysters. "Galveston" trotted along to act as guard.

Jane's red petticoat flag flew bravely over the fort.

Then Jane got a letter. It was sad news.

Her husband had been on his way home to her. Suddenly a Mexican soldier fired a shot at him. James Long was killed instantly.

Now Jane needed money for her family. She asked the government for a pension. Her husband had served in the army. But they refused to give Jane any help.

Now Texas belonged to Mexico. There was a new colony beginning. Stephen F. Austin brought 300 new settlers to Mexican Texas.

Jane wanted to be close to other people, and she moved her family to Austin's colony.

One new settler, Ben Milam, came to bring her husband's clothes. Milam fell ln love with Jane and asked her to marry him.

But Jane said "No!" She would always be in love with one man—James Long.

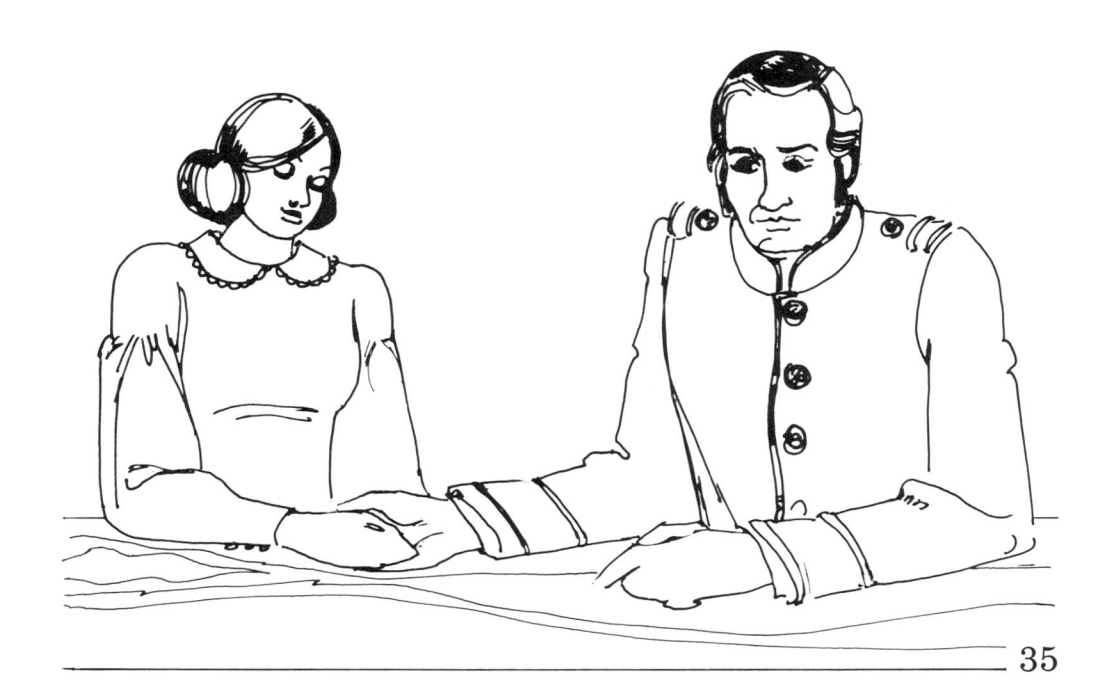

An Innkeeper

Jane was also a good neighbor. People in Austin's colony liked her. She liked them. She and Kian would often pay calls on people who were sick. Jane would bring them tasty food to eat. She would also sit by their bedsides and talk.

Soon Jane's daughter Ann married. Jane was lonely without her.

Then she had an idea. She would open an inn. People would come to eat her good food. She would enjoy their company. Jane's inn was a great success. Then she opened another inn in Brazoria. Both travelers and Texans came to eat there.

One day Jane had a surprise visitor. He was Colonel Juan Almonte. Santa Anna, the head of the Mexican government, sent him to find out what he wanted to know. Would the Texans revolt against Mexico? Santa Anna wanted Texas to remain part of Mexico.

Handsome William Barret Travis also came. He was a newcomer to Texas. Travis was a lawyer, and he helped Jane with her business. He helped her collect money people owed her.

Colonel Almonte wrote to Santa Anna. He said he did not think the Texans would revolt.

But some Texans wanted to be free of Mexico. These Texans often met at Jane's inn. They secretly stored gunpowder there.

Many Texans were ready to fight for their freedom. But others wanted to remain at peace with Mexico.

WAR!

By 1835 many Texans thought Texas should be free. They were angry with Santa Anna.

He refused to support the Constitution, and he refused to meet with Stephen F. Austin.

Austin had gone to Mexico to meet with Santa Anna. But the Mexican leader threw Austin into prison.

Then Santa Anna freed Austin. Now the Texan leader was coming home. The settlers were excited. They wanted to hear what Austin had to say about Santa Anna.

The settlers planned a barbecue and a dance to honor Austin. They decided to hold the party at Jane's inn.

Over 1,000 colonists came to the party. They wanted to hear Austin speak. What would he say about Santa Anna? Would Texas go to war?

Jane and the other colonists listened to Austin. He had been a fine leader of the colony.

Now Austin told the settlers that war might be coming. He called a meeting of the colonists. They had to make plans to defend themselves.

Austin said that most Texans were peaceful farmers. They wanted to remain at peace with Mexico. But they would fight for their rights as free people.

Soon Texans were gathering arms. Santa Anna was on the march. The Texans were planning to fight.

Then Jane met General Sam Houston. He was commander of the Texan army.

Some people said that Jane gave Houston a powder horn for good luck. It had once belonged to the pirate Jean Lafitte.

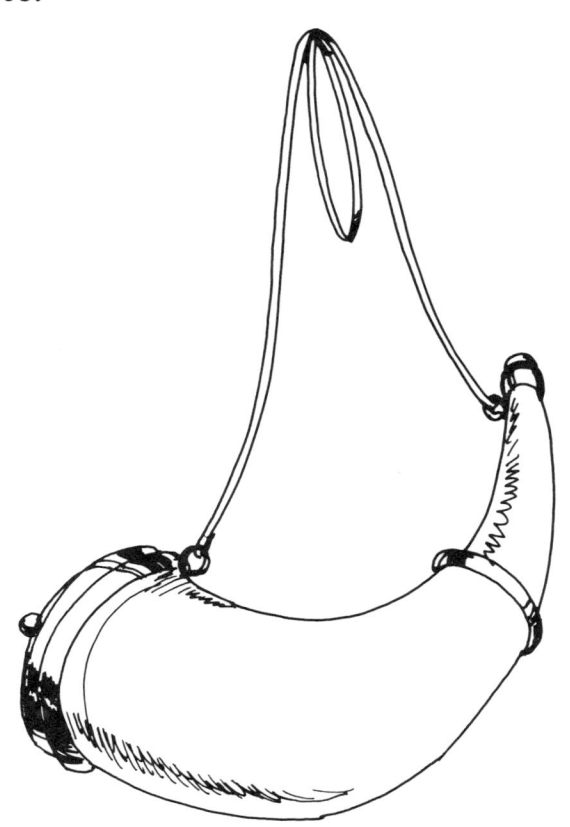

The Texans held another party at Jane's inn. It was in honor of the New Orleans Greys.

These men had come to Texas to fight. They wanted to help the Texans win their freedom.

They believed in liberty. And they wanted land in Texas after the war. They knew the Texans would beat Santa Anna.

Jane met Mirabeau B. Lamar at the party. He had come to Texas from Georgia. He came to the party to speak to the soldiers and the settlers.

Lamar talked about freedom and liberty. He planned to fight for Texas. He wanted to be part of a free Texas.

Other Texans wanted to be free also. They were ready for war.

But many Texans were afraid. Santa Anna was in Texas. He and his army were marching to San Antonio.

Soon news reached the settlers in Austin's colony. The Alamo had fallen. The Texans had lost the battle against Santa Anna. Many brave Texans lay dead.

Many settlers planned to leave Texas. They packed their clothes and hid their household goods.

Jane packed her family's goods also. She and her family joined a group of settlers. They were leaving Texas. Some thought they would never see their homes again.

The journey was a hard one. Many settlers became ill. Some died.

One day as Jane and the other settlers were on the move, they heard shouts. A horseman galloped up.

"Turn back!" he shouted. "Turn back!"

The rider brought good news. General Houston and his troops had won the battle. They had beaten Santa Anna at the battle of San Jacinto.

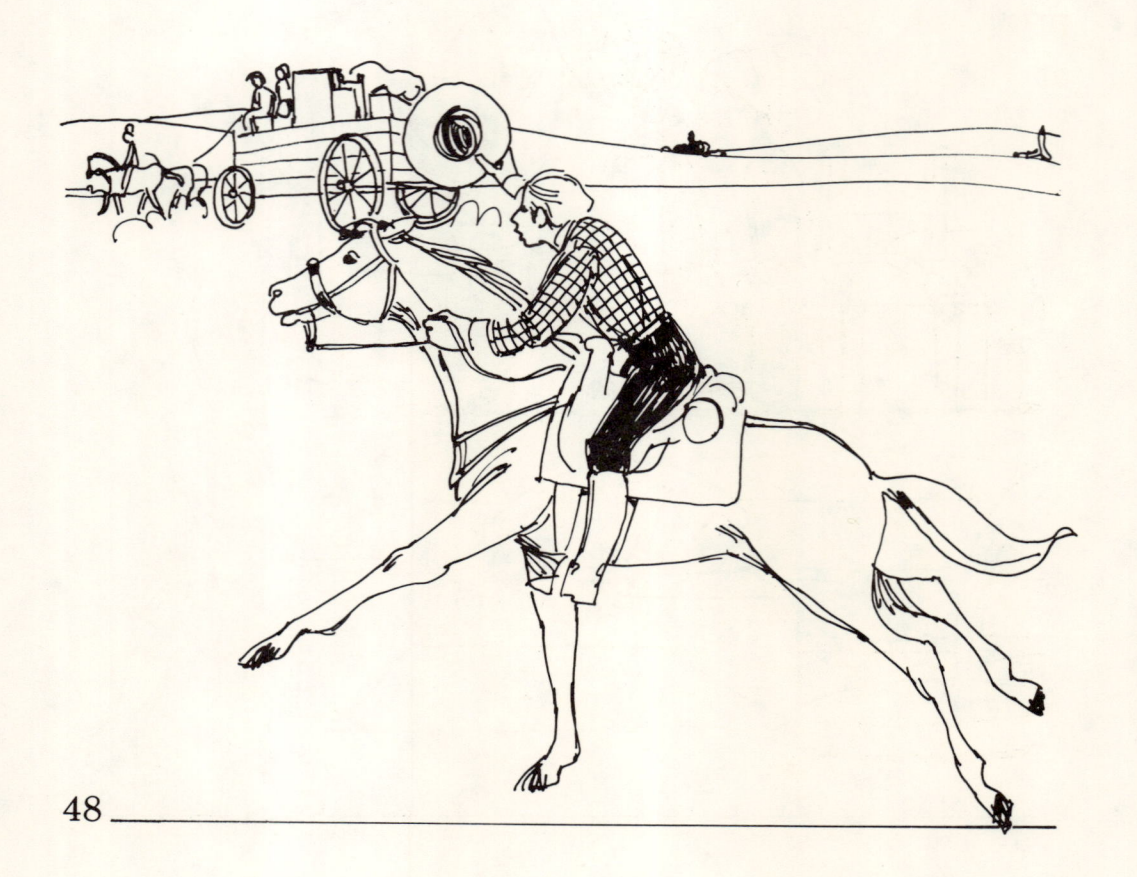

A New Republic

Jane and the settlers were very glad. Now they could return to their homes. Some people found their homes burned. Others found theirs wrecked.

Then Jane made a decision. She would open a hotel in Richmond. Soon her hotel was very busy.

Texas was a new republic, and Sam Houston was president. Many visitors came to Texas, and many stayed at Jane's hotel. Many famous Texans came also.

Sam Houston was the most famous man in Texas. He came to visit Jane's hotel often. Mirabeau Lamar was a hero also. He had fought bravely at the battle of San Jacinto.

Lamar wanted to write a book about James Long. Jane was excited. She worked with Lamar on the book.

Lamar also wrote poetry. He wrote a poem called "Serenade." It was about a beautiful woman called "Bonnie Jane." Everyone knew that Lamar's poem was about Jane Long.

The moon, the cold, chaste moon, my love,
Is riding in the sky;
And like a bridal veil, my love,
The clouds are floating by.
Oh, brighter than that planet, love,
Thy face appears to me;
But when shall I behold its light,
Through bridal drapery?

We owe our gratitude, my love,
To Sol's enlivening ray;
And yet I prize the moonlight, love,
Above the glare of day.
O bonnie Jane, thou art to me
Whate'er in both is best—
Thou art the moonbeam to mine eye,
The sunbeam to my breast.

Jane knew that Lamar was in love with her. When the brave Texan asked her to marry him, Jane said, "No!"

She told him that she would always be true to the memory of James Long.

But she helped Lamar run for president. Houston had served one term as president. Lamar served as the second president of the republic of Texas.

"The Mother of Texas"

Jane was very busy. Her hotel was a great success. Everyone wanted to visit Jane Long's hotel.

Jane became a rich woman. She was able to buy land and several horses.

Jane loved to ride around Richmond in her buggy. She also took long walks. She often took Kian's granddaughter with her. Although Kian had died, Jane was close to her family.

She loved to tell Kian's granddaughter stories of her adventures in early Texas. She told her stories about her grandmother's bravery. She told her stories of how she and Kian had fooled the Indians.

People in Texas knew who Jane Long was. They nodded to her. Men bowed when she passed by. They called her "Aunt Jane" or "Grandma Long."

Many called her "The Mother of Texas." Jane had a very special place in the hearts of Texans.

Then Texas was at war again. Texas joined other southern states to fight in the Civil War. Jane's grandson joined other Texans. He marched off to fight for the South against the North. Jane was also loyal to the South. She believed the South would win the war.

She knitted socks for the soldiers. She also sent boxes of clothing to the troops.

But the South lost the war, and Jane was very sad. Still Texas was a great state.

Now Jane was growing old. The "Mother of Texas" was growing tired.

One day she and Kian's granddaughter set out in the buggy. They rode around the town of Richmond. Jane said "goodbye" to everyone she knew. She took one last look at the town and the state she loved.

Then Jane went to visit an ice-cream parlor. She enjoyed one last dish of her favorite ice-cream.

How good it tasted to her. She remembered her lonely Christmas at Bolivar Point. She remembered when she and Kian had only fish to eat.

Christmas came. It was a festive time for everyone. Jane spent her last Christmas with her family. She told stories of early days in Texas.

When Jane Long died on December 30, 1880, she was buried in Richmond. She was buried where many Texas heroes lay. Many people wrote stories about Jane. They wrote about "The Mother of Texas." They wrote about the young girl who came to Texas and found adventure. And they honored the brave woman that Jane was.

Words to Know

frontier	trotted	peace
adventure	bend	constitution
empire	petticoat	barbecue
traitor	settlers	defend
plot	venison	alarmed
backgammon	instantly	commander
niece	pension	powderhorn
guardian	colony	pirate
merchant	colonist	liberty
explorers	neighbor	journey
neutral	government	decision
fringe	revolt	republic
belongings	inn	poetry
oysters	newcomer	president
whined	lawyer	troops
pallet	gunpowder	state
barrel	freedom	remember

BOOKS ABOUT JANE LONG AND HER LIFE IN TEXAS

Author, *Title,* Publisher

Crawford, *New Life, New Land: Women in Early Texas,* Eakin
Crawford and Ragsdale, *Women In Texas,* Eakin
Exley, *Texas Tears and Texas Sunshine,* Texas A&M Press
Hogan, *The Texas Republic,* University of Texas Press
McDonald, *Travis,* Jenkins
Pickrell, *Pioneer Women in Texas,* Pemberton Press
Ramsey, *Thunder Beyond the Brazos,* Eakin
Turner, *The Life and Times of Jane Long,* Texian Press